The Lord
Is My
Shepherd

The Lord Is My Shepherd

Inspiration for Couples

Carol Lynn Pearson

GIBBS SMITH
TO ENRICH AND INSPIRE HUMANKIND
Salt Lake City | Charleston | Santa Fe | Santa Barbara

First Edition
13 12 11 10 09   5 4 3 2 1

Text © 2009 Carol Lynn Pearson

Published by
Gibbs Smith
P.O. Box 667
Layton, Utah 84041

1.800.835.4993 orders
www.gibbs-smith.com

Designed and produced by Ron Stucki
Printed and bound in Canada
Gibbs Smith books are printed on either recycled, 100% post-
consumer waste, FSC-certified papers or on paper produced from
a 100% certified sustainable forest/controlled wood source.

Library of Congress Cataloging-in-Publication Data

Pearson, Carol Lynn.
   The Lord is my shepherd : inspiration for couples /
Carol Lynn Pearson. — 1st ed.
      p. cm.
   ISBN-13: 978-1-4236-0586-7
   ISBN-10: 1-4236-0586-1
   I. Bible. O.T. Psalms XXIII—Meditations. 2. Spouses—
Prayers and devotions. I. Title.
   BS145023rd .P43 2009
   242'.5—dc22
                              2009000470

THE
TWENTY-THIRD
PSALM

A Psalm of David

The Lord is my shepherd; I shall not want.

He maketh me to lie down in green pastures.
He leadeth me beside the still waters.
He restoreth my soul.

He leadeth me in the paths of righteousness
for his name's sake.
Yea, though I walk through the valley
of the shadow of death,
I will fear no evil
For thou art with me.
Thy rod and thy staff, they comfort me.

Thou preparest a table before me in the presence
of mine enemies.
Thou anointest my head with oil.
My cup runneth over.

Surely goodness and mercy shall follow me
all the days of my life
And I will dwell in the house of the Lord
forever.

Dear Lord my Shepherd,

I am a spouse, lover, partner, friend.
I have committed to assist you in
Shepherding one of the dearest of your flock.

My sweetheart's value is without price.
My abilities are imperfect.

Teach me to care for my love as you care for us all.
I read the pattern of your perfect care
In the words of King David
Royal shepherd of Palestine.

Help me to follow your lead.

The Lord
Is My
Shepherd

This is not a question, my love.
It is a declaration
A fact forever:

The Lord *is* our shepherd!

I *am* your spouse, lover, partner, friend.

No "ifs," no hidden clauses.
You are not here on approval.
I have already approved.

From every other I chose you
And my commitment is absolute.

I will be here with you
For you
Until the end of my days
And, I hope, beyond.

You are a given in my life
And you are a gift.

From every other I chose you

We come together as equals.
Still, I have been made
  my lover's keeper.
I have been made steward of your joy.

I have been called to
Reverence you with my mind
Celebrate you with my body
And honor you with my soul.

I have been asked to create
A home for your heart
As small and warm as an embrace.

I have been consecrated
The one who will care for you
Through every storm.

I have been made shepherd
  to our relationship
Assigned to keep a clear and constant eye
  on its well-being
To bring provisions for its growth.

We come together as equals

12

I will learn from the Master
    to be a good shepherd.

I am not yet perfect.
But I am yours.

I am yours

I Shall
Not Want

For want of a nail the shoe was lost.
For want of a shoe the horse was lost.
For want of a horse the rider was lost . . ."

And finally the kingdom was lost.

For want of attention
So many marriages
So many lovely love stories are lost.

It is my commitment that ours
Will not be among them.

To the best of my ability:

You will not want for adoration.
You will daily hear the words
"I love you, I love you."

You will daily know the touch of a hand
That would rather feel your skin
Than gold.

I love you, I love you

You will daily see my eyes
    reflect your face
As the newest wonder of the world.

You will not want
For time and space to be alone
To remember the richness of solitude.

And surely you will never want for company.
Even in my absence
    you will feel the presence
Of my love.

You will not want for security.
You will know that my word is sure
And that deceiving you
    and deceiving the Lord
To me are one.

You will not want
For an occasional rose or book or poem
Or something silly to make you laugh.

You will not want

You will not want for someone
To pray daily for your happiness
To gratefully, proudly watch you thrive

Today
Tomorrow
And always.

Today, tomorrow, and always

He Maketh
Me to Lie
Down in
Green Pastures

Sheep are seldom still.
The shepherd starts them grazing
    about four in the morning.
By ten the sun is hot and the stomach of the sheep
Is full of undigested food.
So the shepherd makes the sheep lie down
    in a green pasture.
The sheep will not eat lying down
So it rests and chews its cud
And digests
And, perhaps, enjoys.

Your days are filled with work, my love,
As are mine.
Like the sheep, we are seldom still.
I would like our home to be a green pasture
Where along with celebration
There can be meditation.
May the business of our lives
Find its proper place.

Our home will be a green pasture

May it not spill over constantly
Into our green pasture of repose.
Green is the color of nature, fertility, life
Of growth, balance, harmony.

I want to see you walk through our door and sigh
And feel some weight slip away
Because here is home and your spirit
    can lie down safely
Breathe more deeply.

And at day's end
May we two be the lovers spoken of by Solomon
Son of the shepherd-psalmist David:
"How fair is thy love, my spouse!
How much better is thy love than wine!
And the smell of thine ointments than all spices.
Behold thou art fair, my love;
Thou hast doves' eyes.
Behold thou art fair;
Also our bed is green."

How fair is thy love, my spouse

In the green pasture of our bed
May we only love
And rest
And dream.

May we only love, and rest, and dream

He Leadeth
Me Beside the
Still Waters

The shepherd leads
Walking confidently at the head of the flock
And the sheep follow.

He leads to find still waters
For sheep will not drink
From waters that are turbulent.

The shepherd does not drive from behind
Forcing and frightening the flock.
He leads.

You and I, my love
Take turns leading and following
In a dance of our own design.
In your specialties, you lead
As I do in mine.

I know that we seek to control
When we fail to inspire.
In my leading I wish only to inspire you.

You and I take turns in a
dance of our own design

Demands, threats, anger—
Those are not still waters.

Encouragement, suggestion, calm request—
We both drink deep and are refreshed.

There is no keeping my delight or
    my sadness from you.
My emotions are in the air between us
Like dust or oxygen
And you breathe them.

My peace takes you to still waters
My distress to troubled ones.
I would be a pool of peace for you, my love
An oasis in your day.

I will honor you with my feelings.
My grief I will not keep from you.
But I will not live in my fears
For there is a Shepherd who guides us both
And in him do I trust.

I will honor you with my feelings

Then let our journey be a dance of joy
Leading and following
Finding and sharing those sweet, still waters.

Let our journey be a dance of joy

He Restoreth
My Soul

Your soul, my love, is the breath of God
And I am its guardian.
I see it soar
I see it sink.

And when the blows of this world
Take your godly breath away
When I read doubt or defeat in your eyes
When I see your soul suffer—

I will help restore it
With an encouraging word:

"You are wonderful and you are deeply loved."

"I am so proud of you."

"Yes, you can. Of course you can!"

"You are the best!"

Or with a listening that says nothing
And says everything.

Your soul is the breath of God

And surely with that sweet prerogative of lovers—
An embrace of hands
And lips
And heart.

Should you do things to damage your soul
I will help with the repair
Reminding you always of who you really are.

Even the psalmist David
Turned from his godliness and did wrong.
He was without strength and turned again to the Lord
Who restored his soul.

Out in the pasture when a sheep unfortunately
Finds itself on its back, feet in the air
It is a "cast" sheep.
It cannot right itself and will die if not noticed.
It is the shepherd's job to notice
To come to the sheep without blame or shame
And gently right it
Restoring it to its place in the flock.

An embrace of hands,
and lips, and heart

Should you ever be so cast down
That you are unable to right yourself
I will notice.
I will invoke the Master Shepherd
I will invoke others who love you.
We will come to you
And you will be encircled by care
However long it may take
Until your soul is restored.

You will be encircled by care

He Leadeth Me
in the Paths
of Righteousness
for His
Name's Sake

With several flocks at a watering hole
The time comes for leaving.

Each shepherd calls
And each sheep responds
Separating itself out from the group
Following the voice it trusts.

You know my voice, my love,
And I believe that you trust it.

I commit to be worthy of that trust.
I will try to influence you
Only into right paths
Never into paths that serve me
But do not serve you.
(And I know that no path truly serves me
That does not also serve you.)
Let us lead one another along the route
Marked by the Master Shepherd.

Let us lead one another

31

Still, I pledge to remember that *paths*
    is a plural word
And that as we travel
Your paths will differ from mine in wonderful ways
That I must encourage and celebrate.

Finally I promise to remember
That my compass is not perfect
And that the only sure direction
    in which I can point you
Goes not out there
But in here
Into that rich, private terrain of your heart
That kingdom of God within you.

There
You hear the Lord's voice
The wise voice of your own soul
That knows the way and leads you always
In right paths for his name's sake.

I pledge, I promise

As you follow your soul
And I follow mine
Surely our journey will lead us to joy.

Our journey will lead us to joy

Yea, Though
I Walk through
the Valley
of the Shadow
of Death,
I Will Fear
No Evil

In the Holy Land there is a place called
"The Valley of the Shadow of Death."
It is south of the Jericho Road
Leading from Jerusalem to the Dead Sea
A mountain pass that shepherds named
Because of its steep sides, sheer rock walls
Caves and crevices that might hide animals of prey.

The change of seasons made it necessary
To move the sheep to the high country
Through this terrifying pass.

I have been called to travel through that dark place
More than once, my love,
    and I know you have as well.
The Lord our Shepherd was with us
As were friends who warmed us
Walked with us
And kept us from looking down.

Now we have one another.

We have one another

When you have a personal call
To enter that demanding valley
I promise that you will not travel it alone.

The Lord our Shepherd will be with you.
I will be with you.
I will hold you, love you, weep with you
Protect and guide you as best I can.

And when we find that our love itself
Has entered that dark valley
Whether from our neglect
Or from a calling
To take our relationship to higher ground
I will do my best to shepherd it through
     without judgment
With only the greatest of care.

I will remind us both that it is only
The *shadow* of death that we meet—
A dark pretender.

I will hold you, love you, weep with you

I will also insist we remember, my love,
That we are to walk *through* this dark valley
Not make our home here
Asking our love to live on the ragged weeds
Of grief and resentment and fear.

We will walk *through* the valley,
    as sure-footed as we can
Reaching the high country
Where there is sun and clear water and birds
And the greenest of pastures.

We will walk as sure-footed as we can

For Thou Art
with Me

Did you notice, my love?
Something remarkable happened in these five words.
"He" became "Thou"!
The psalmist no longer speaks *of* the Shepherd
But *to* the Shepherd
As he does for the rest of the verse.

A heart, I think, broke open.
The Valley of the Shadow of Death will do that.

When the path is dark and narrow
Or a storm is raging
The sheep instinctively draw closer to the shepherd.
A new intimacy is born.
No longer "He," over there
But "Thou," here.

When I first saw you weep
I saw you differently
And I loved you more.

I saw you differently and
I loved you more

I promise that whatever dark valley you enter
Or our relationship enters
I will ever be aware of the divine "thou"
Of your being
Never see you as object
But as powerful subject in your own sentence.

For those times when it is my turn to weep
In the dark valley
I know the Lord and thou
Are with me
Two loves to lean upon.

I ask you now:
On my final journey
Through the Valley of the Shadow of Death
Shepherd me.
Hold me and say—

"My love
There is purpose to this path.

The Lord and thou: two
loves to lean upon

You have been led here.
Look up, not down.

This path leads to the high country
Where there is sun and clear water and birds
And the greenest of pastures.
Soon I will meet you there."

I will meet you

Thy Rod and
Thy Staff,
They Comfort
Me

From ancient days
The shepherd has carried two things:
A rod, which is a club
And a staff, a long, slender stick
　　with a hook on one end.

I carry these too, every day
And I pray to use them only
　　for the comfort of my love.

I have used the rod
Never against you, never, never that.
But like the shepherd David
　　who used his rod to attack
The lion and the bear that came to raid his flocks
I have raised my rod against predators.

I have kept watch by night and by day
And I have seen dangers approach:
People, ideas, temptations
That would raid and devour the sanctity of our bond.

For the comfort of my love

I have stood firm against their attack
And I will stand firm again.
You can sleep undisturbed
Knowing I am a sentinel ever watchful
And charged with the safety of our love.
And this for your comfort.

The staff is used for guiding sheep
Into a new path
Or along a dangerous and difficult route.
The tip is laid against the animal's side
With gentle pressure.

Marriages collapse from coercion.
I pray for the wisdom to use my staff well
Use it only for encouragement.

I hope to press you gently toward your chosen goals
Not toward mine.
I pledge to cherish your freedom
Even knowing you are free to leave me

I pledge to cherish your freedom

And hoping that very knowledge
Binds you closer.

This will be my mantra
And the measure of each decision:
For your comfort.
Always for your comfort.

Always for your comfort

Thou Preparest
a Table
before Me in the
Presence of
Mine Enemies

The high mountain country of the summer ranges
Were known as "tablelands."

Even before the snow had melted
The shepherd took great pains
To prepare this rough country for his flock
Plucking poisonous weeds by the root
    and burning them
Distributing salt and minerals
Clearing out the watering holes
Repairing small dams he had made the year before
Tracking or trapping mountain lions
Or bears or other predators.

When he was finished—
A table prepared for his flock.

I would prepare a space that will nourish our love
Not just let it range here and there
Making do.

*I would prepare a space
to nourish our love*

I will prepare the day so there is time for sweetness.
I will give hours to purchase a living
But not all the hours.
Some I will hoard and spend on love.

I will prepare my mind, settle concerns
So they do not sap the energy of intimacy.

I will walk the landscape of my heart
Pluck out by the roots
Resentments that poison the waters.
I will distribute the salt of forgiveness and of humor
Repair the reservoirs of appreciation.

I will prepare my body
Ensure the scent and sense of invitation
Warm, warm, a home for your desire.

Even in the presence of our enemies
Imperfection and deterioration:
Thinning hair, cellulite, illness
Forgetfulness and insensitivity—

A home for your desire

Yes, even in the presence of complacency
Misunderstanding
And occasional stupidity
I will prepare a table for my love
The best I can manage
Mind, heart, body.

I will light a candle
Smile
Open my arms
And invite you to the blessed feast.

Mind, heart, body

Thou Anointest My Head with Oil

At the first sign of flies, of parasites,
    of bramble scratches
Or injury of any kind to the head of the sheep
The shepherd applies a balm,
    a remedy of olive oil
Often mixed with sulphur and spices—
Not unlike the anointing given to the traveler
By the Good Samaritan who poured oil
    into his wounds.

Immediately the troubled sheep becomes content.

I have tended your occasional wound
With balm from the drugstore.
But I would give you blessing that goes inches
Past skin into soul.

I hope to observe the wounds of your heart
And bring the sweet oil of kindness there.
Never turning away or crossing the road
I would be your resident Good Samaritan.

*I will bring the sweet oil of kindness
to the wounds of your heart*

I would anoint you, too, my honored guest
With customary oil poured upon your head
Anoint you to become the royal one
That you are in the kingdom of God.

David was anointed king long before he became one.
I can do that for you.
I need no container or substance.
I anoint you with my vision
With my voice, my touch, my kiss.

I pledge to see you
Even in bad times
Through mistakes, failures, angry words
Disappointments—
See you as the anointed one
Dedicated to the service of God
The special one
A duplicate of which the world has never seen.
In Hebrew "messiah" means "the anointed one."
I anoint you with my belief
That your special gifts are helping
    to redeem this world.

*I anoint you with my voice,
my touch, my kiss*

And I give constant gratitude that
Your gifts bless me.

I hold the image of your divinity.
I have authority.
I am your appointed spouse
And you are my anointed one.

Your gifts bless me

My Cup
Runneth
Over

After David brought his flock in for the night
And anointed the sheep's injuries with oil
He dipped a cup into a large earthen jar of water
Bringing it out, never half full, but overflowing.

He then set it before the sheep
Who would sink its nose into the water
Clear to its eyes
And drink deeply until refreshed.

The Lord our Shepherd does that for us too
And his cup overflows.

We look at our lives
Compare them to the lives we anticipated
Or the lives around us
And we try to decide whether the cup is half empty
Or the cup is half full.

All the while the cup is overflowing.

Drink deeply until refreshed

I have learned that the only thing missing
From any situation
    is what I have failed to bring to it.
And I fail to bring only what I do not realize I have
For the Lord is my shepherd and I want for nothing.

Like the miraculous jar of oil that does not run out
For the widow who fed Elijah
Our source never runs dry.

I would be as generous as that jar of oil, my love.
I would be for you a friend, a lover, a spouse
Who is never spent
Whose patience, kindness, wisdom, humor
Bubble over the brim.
But I am a cup that often feels empty
And my edges are sometimes dry and sharp.
Occasionally I am a desert.

Yet this I know:
The remedy for emptiness is appreciation.
When I find one thing about my life,
    about myself, about you

I would be a friend, a lover, a spouse

To appreciate, it invites another and another
And then, like magic, the cup expands and—
Such abundance:
Good measure, pressed down, shaken together
    and running over!

And this I can promise:
When I have little to give
I will go to my source and drink
Do something I enjoy
Spend a few moments listening to my heart
Breathe deep and let go of everything but now
Feel the cup overflow
And spill some joy on you as you come in the door.

I will spill some joy on you

Surely Goodness
and Mercy
Shall Follow Me
All the Days
of My Life

What a wonderful word, surely.
Not maybe, not probably.
Surely!

Just as sheep follow the shepherd
Because there is an affinity between them
So qualities and experiences and people follow us.

What we have become sings its own song
Vibrates like a tuning fork
And is answered by its equal.

This is what I want for you and for our relationship:
Goodness and mercy.
I would wrap our love in goodness and mercy
Feed it goodness and mercy
Until it sings and everyone around
    can hear the sounds
Of goodness and mercy.

From everywhere then will come the echoes
The sweet followers

*I would wrap our love in
goodness and mercy*

The thoughts, experiences, rewards
Of that exceptional couple
Goodness and mercy.

I will practice first with myself
As giving all to you and nothing to me
Is not good.
Forgiving you and finding fault with me
Is not merciful.

I will anoint myself with the oil of gladness
Serve myself from a full table
That I might have and give life more abundantly.

And when I forget or fail
Then I receive mercy from you and mercy from me.

This is a wonderful dance we do
The four of us:
Leading and following
You, me, and the promised

I will anoint myself with
the oil of gladness

Goodness and mercy that will follow us
Follow our love
Surely, surely
All the days of our lives.

Goodness and mercy will follow our love

And I Will
Dwell in
the House
of the Lord
Forever

Such a journey this has been
Through the words of David's psalm:
The Lord our Shepherd in the field
Is now our gracious host in his house
And we his honored guests
Not for one night of hospitality
But forever.

The house of love that you and I have built
Is a starter home patterned after
That celestial abode.

We have built on holy ground.
We are whole apart from each other
But together we are even more whole
And more holy.

I pledge to do careful upkeep of our home.
I pledge to see you, my love,
As an honored guest in my heart
And in our home
Staying always on watch to serve you.

We have built a house of
love on holy ground

I pledge to be a host to the Lord as well
Inviting him to our table
Learning at his feet.

In this way
Our house will become his house.
And when we change residence from our house to his
Move into the mansion on high
Held for us in escrow
Perhaps we will hardly know the difference.

We will dwell with one another
And we will dwell with him
Both here and there
Both now and then
On earth and in heaven
In the house of the Lord
Today and forever.

We will dwell with one another in
the house of the Lord forever